Growing Up!

Ginger the Kitten

by Jane Burton

Purnell

A Purnell Book

First published in Great Britain in 1988 by Macdonald & Co (Publishers) Ltd
Greater London House, Hampstead Road, London NW1 7QX
A BPCC plc company

in association with Belitha Press Limited
31 Newington Green, London N16 9PU

Copyright © in this format Belitha Press Limited 1988
Text and photographs copyright © Jane Burton 1988
Conceived, designed and produced by Belitha Press Limited 1988
Art Director: Treld Bicknell
ISBN 0-361-07856-0 (hardback)
ISBN 0-361-07857-9 (paperback)

Printed in Hong Kong.

*Ginger also appeared with his family in NINE LIVES by Jane Burton and
Michael Allaby, published by Ebury Press, 1985*

Snorkel is giving birth to another litter of kittens. Barley, the first to be born, is nearly an hour old, and already dry.

Ginger is the fifth kitten in the litter. He is only a few minutes old, and his fur is still wet. Snorkel will lick him clean and dry before his next two brothers are born.

Snorkel settles herself comfortably, purring loudly and snorting, which she does when she is especially pleased. Her seven new kittens have found her teats and are suckling contentedly.

Five days old

Very young kittens sleep nearly all the time. They cannot see or hear because their eyes and ears are closed. It is hard to tell if Ginger is asleep or awake. Though tiny and toothless, he will snarl like a wild cat if he smells a stranger.

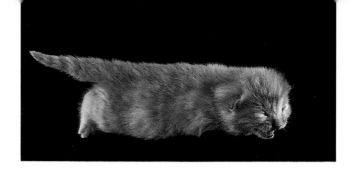

Seven days old

Ginger has wandered out of the nest and is not happy to be all by himself. He mews loudly and pushes himself along on his tummy. He cannot see, but he can find his way by smell, and by feeling with his whiskers and chin and paws.

When he finds Barley and his sister Tabitha, he is happy again. He pushes underneath them for warmth. Snorkel will carry them back to the nest.

Ten days old

Ginger's eyes have opened. Now he can see, but not very well. Probably he can only just tell light from dark.

Three weeks old

Ginger can toddle along quite strongly with his tummy off the ground, but mostly he stays warmly in the nest with all his brothers and his sister, Tabitha.

Four weeks old

The kittens start to venture out of the nest when only one month old. They begin to sample solid food and to use their litter tray. They are getting playful.

Five weeks old

Ginger pounces on a woolly ball and grabs it with his teeth and claws. He rolls over and dabs at it with a paw to make it roll away so he can chase and catch it again.

Six weeks old

The kittens play outdoors when the weather is warm. They race after each other through the grass. Ginger pounces on Barley's tail and grabs it, but the tail slips through his paws.

Barley turns on Ginger and they roll over and over together, boxing with their front paws and kicking at each other. Kitten games prepare them for real fights when they are grown up.

On another adventure Ginger and two brothers
explore along a railing. Ginger pauses to sharpen
his claws by scratching at the rough bark. As he
works his claws in and out, little pieces flake off
from the tips, and this keeps them needle-sharp.
Even at this age kittens balance perfectly on such

a narrow pole. They have no fear of falling. If one should slip, it can cling on with its sharp claws and scramble back up again. Or it can let go and drop to the ground. As it falls, a cat can twist its body so that it lands the right way up, on its feet, unhurt.

Seven weeks old

The kittens hungrily tuck in to a large plate of catfood. They are growing fast, so need a lot to eat. They have quite nice table manners for kittens, and never growl or lash out at each other when feeding, as some kitten families do.

When each kitten has had enough to eat, it politely moves away to lick its paws and wash its face. Ginger is the last to stop eating. He looks up from the empty plate as if asking for more, but he is full up, really.

Eight weeks old

The kittens' favourite indoor playground is a tattered old chair. Each time they play on it, the chair gets more shredded. They climb on it, sharpen their claws on it, chew it and unravel it.

Ginger has had enough romping and is ready to settle down for a nap. His eyes are still kitten-blue, but soon they will be turning yellow.

Ten weeks old

The kittens have discovered the pond. Ginger walks carefully along the parapet, out towards the middle.

He tries to get to the other side by walking across the floating pondweed. Quickly he scrambles back onto the parapet, feet wet and tail dripping. He and Fred seem to be marooned in the middle of the pond. But Ginger soon realizes that he can cross the water by jumping. Fred turns round and walks back the way they came!

Three months old

Fergus, Ginger's father, is usually prowling in the woods by himself. Today, he has stayed at home. He washes Ginger's face in a friendly way, but Ginger is a bit scared of him and ready to leap away.

The kittens go everywhere now, and spend all day exploring. Bushes are miniature jungles in which they prowl like tiny tigers. Ginger lurks, half hidden among the dappled shadows, ready to spring out on one of his unsuspecting brothers.

Ginger can leap up onto the railings and balance on the smallest and highest point. He is graceful and sure-footed and can jump lightly down whenever he wants to.

Four months old

Kittens are born climbers – they can climb as soon as they can walk. As they grow bigger, they climb higher and higher. Tree-climbing is very important to cats, because if an enemy chases them on the ground they can escape by rushing up the nearest tree. Cats also climb just for fun, as Ginger and Barley are climbing the old apple tree. Going up the thick trunk is kittens' play; there are plenty of knobs and twiggy branches for pawholds.

Ginger balances perfectly as he explores the branches, always looking upwards – never down.

He climbs effortlessly, higher and higher. His
supple body twists and stretches as he climbs, and
his curved claws cling to the rough bark.

Nearly at the top of the tree Barley joins him.
Suddenly it seems a long way down to the ground.
It is always much more difficult for cats to climb
down again, because they cannot go down
headfirst holding on with their back feet, like a
squirrel can. Ginger has to let himself down
backwards, or jump down. It takes Ginger and
Barley very much longer to scramble down than
it took them to climb up.

Six months old

Now that Ginger is a grown cat, he goes on the prowl through the wild woods a long way from home. He is alert to every tiny sound or movement. Anything that moves or rustles, he pounces on.

Pausing to sniff a blade of dead grass, he studies the scent left on it by another cat – one of his brothers, perhaps. His stripy coat blends with the russet colours of the dead ferns and fallen leaves. Soon the trees will be bare. They are getting ready for the winter.

Nine months old

Ginger is a big handsome cat now. The winter
has come. Out of doors it is cold and wet, so
Ginger stays indoors in the warm, sleeping and
eating and polishing his paws. If snow comes, he
might be tempted out to play with the falling
snowflakes. Then, in the mild days of spring, he
will be out once again, playing in the garden with
his brothers or prowling through the woods alone.